Charles Godfrey Leland

Hans Breitmann's Party

With other ballads

Charles Godfrey Leland

Hans Breitmann's Party
With other ballads

ISBN/EAN: 9783744789431

Printed in Europe, USA, Canada, Australia, Japan

Cover: Foto ©Thomas Meinert / pixelio.de

More available books at **www.hansebooks.com**

Hans Breitmann's Party.

With other Ballads.

By Charles G. Leland.

New and Enlarged Edition.

PHILADELPHIA:

T. B. PETERSON & BROTHERS;

306 CHESTNUT STREET.

RINGWALT & BROWN, PRE.

Contents.

———————

Ad Musam.

"Est mihi schoena etenim et praestanti corpore liebsta:
Haec sola est mea Musa meoque regieril in Herzo,
Huic me ergebo ipsum meeque illi abstatto geluebda,
Huic ehrensaulas aufrichto optroque Geschenka,
Hic etiam absiugo liedros et carmina scribo."

Rapsodia Andra, Leipzig, 17th century.

(4)

Hans Breitmann's Party.

HANS BREITMANN gife a barty,
    Dey had biano-blayin;
    I felled in lofe mit a Merican frau,
Her name vas Madilda Yane.
She hat haar as prown ash a pretzel,
    Her eyes vas himmel-plue,
Und ven dey looket indo mine,
    Dey shplit mine heart in two.

Hans Breitmann gife a barty,
    I vent dere you'll pe pound.
I valtzet mit Madilda Yane
    Und vent shpinnen round und round.
De pootiest Fraeulein in de House,
    She vayed 'pout dwo hoondred pound,
Und efery dime she gife a shoomp
    She make de vindows sound.

Hans Breitmann gife a barty,
    I dells you it cost him dear.
Dey rolled in more ash sefen kecks
    Of foost-rate Lager Beer.
Und venefer dey knocks de shpicket in
    De Deutschers gifes a cheer.
I dinks dat so vine a barty,
    Nefer coom to a het dis year.

Hans Breitmann gife a barty;
　Dere all vas Souse und Brouse,
Ven de sooper comed in, de gompany
　Did make demselfs to house;
Dey ate das Brot and Gensy broost,
　De Bratwurst and Braten fine,
Und vash der Abendessen down
　Mit four parrels of Neckarwein.

Hans Breitmann gife a barty
　We all cot troonk ash bigs.
I poot mine mout to a parrel of bier
　Und emptied it oop mit a schwigs.
Und denn I gissed Madilda Yane
　Und she shlog me on de kop,
Und de gompany fited mit daple-lecks
　Dill de coonshtable made oos shtop.

Hans Breitmann gife a barty—
　Where ish dat barty now!
Where ish de lofely golden cloud
　Dat float on de moundain's prow?
Where ish de himmelstrahlende Stern—
　De shtar of de shpirit's light?
All goned afay mit de Lager Beer—
　Afay in de ewigkeit!

Breitmann in Battle.

" Tunc tapfre ausfuhrere Streitum et Rittris dignum
potuere erjagere lobum."

DER FADER UND DER SON.

dinks I'll go a fitin—outspoke der Breitemann,
" It's eighdeen hoonderd fordy eight since I kits
   swordt in hand ;
Dese fourdeen years mit Hecker all roostin I haf been,
Boot now I kicks der Teufel oop and goes for
   sailin in."

" If you go land out-ridin," said Caspar Pickletongue,
" Foost ding you knows you cooms across some repels
   prave and young,
Away down Sout' in Tixey, dey'll split you like a
   clam"—
" For dat," spoke out der Breitmann, " I doos not
   gare one tam !"

Who der Teufel pe's de repels und vhere dey kits deir
   sass,
If dey make a run on Breitmann he'll soon let out de
   gas ;
I'll shplit dem like kartoffels : I'll slog em on de kop ;
I'll set de plackguarts roonin so dey don't know vhere
   to shtop."

(7)

Und den outshpoke der Breitmann, mit his schlaeger py
    his side :
" Forvarts, my pully landsmen ! it's dime to run und
    ride ;
Will riden, will fighten—der Copitain I'll pe,   [rie !"
It's sporn und horn und saddle now—all in de Cavall-

Und ash dey rode troo Winchester, so herrlich to pe
    scen,
Dere coomed some repel cavallrie a riden on de creen ;
Mit a sassy repel Dootchman—an colonel in gommand :
Says he, " Vot Teufel makes you here in dis mein
    Faderland ?

" You're dressed oop like a shentleman mit your plack-
    guard Yankee crew,
You mudsills and meganics ! Der Teufel put you troo !
Old Yank you ought to shtay at home und dake your
    liddle horn,
Mit some oldt roomans for a noorse"—der Breitmann
    laugh mit shkorn.

" Und should I trink mein lager-bier und roost mine
    self to home ?   [thoom :
Ife got too many dings like you to mash beneat' my
In many a fray und fierce foray dis Deutschman will be
    feared   [his peard."
Pefore he stops dis vightin trade—'twas dere he greyed

" I pools dat peard out by de roots—I gifes him sooch
    a dwist   [tionist !
Dill all de plood roons out, you tamned old Apoli-
Your creenpacks mit your swordt und watch right ofer
    you moost shell,   [h—ll !"
Und den you goes to Libby straight—und after dat to

" Mein creenpacks und mein schlaeger, I kits 'em in
    New York,   [talk ;"
To gife dem up to creenhorns, young man, is not de
De heroes shtopped deir sassin' here und grossed deir
    sabres dwice,
Und de vay dese Deutschers vent to vork vos von pig
    ding on ice.

Der younger fetch de older such a gottallmachty smack
Der Breitmann dinks he really hears his skool go shplit
    und crack ;
Der repel choomps dwelfe paces back, und so he safe
    his life :
Der Breitmann says : " I guess dem choomps you
    learns dem of your vife."

"If I should learn of romans I dinks it vere a shame,
Bei Gott I am a shentleman, aristograt, and game.
My fader vos anoder—I lose him fery young—
Ter teufel take your soul ! Coom on ! I'll split your
    waggin' tongue !"

A Yankee drick der Breitmann dried—dat oldt gray-
    pearded man—   [he ran.
For ash the repel raised his swordt, bencat' dat swordt
All roundt der shlim yoong repel's waist his arms oldt
    Breitmann pound,
Und shlinged him down oopon his pack und laidt him
    on der ground.

" Who rubs against olt kittle-pots may keep vite—if he
    can,   [man ?
Say vot you dinks of vightin now mit dis old shentle-
Your dime is oop; you got to die, und I your breest
    vill pe ;
Peliev'st dou in Morál Ideas ? If so I lets you free."

" I don't know nix apout Ideas—no more dan pout
    Saint Paul,
Since I peen down in Tixey I kits no books at all ;
I'm greener ash de clofer-grass ; I'm shtupid as a
    shpoon ;
I'm ignoranter ash de nigs—for dey takes de *Tribune.*

" Mein fader's name vas Breitmann, I heard mein mut-
    ter say,
She read de bapers dat he died after she rooned afay ;
Dey say he leaf some broperty—berhaps 'twas all a
    sell—
If I could lay mein hands on it I likes it mighty well."

" Und vas dy fader Breitmann? *Bist du* his kit und kin ?
Denn know dat *ich* der Breitmann dein lieber Vater bin?"
Der Breitmann poolled his hand-shoe off und shooked
    him py de hand;
" Ve'll hafe some trinks on strengt of dis—or else may
    I po tam'd !"

" Oh ! fader, how I shlog your kop," der younger
    Breitmann said ;
" I'd den dimes sooner had it coom right down on mine
    own headt !"
" Oh, never mind—dat soon dry oop—I shticks him mit
    a blaster ;   [der."
If I had shplit you like a fish, dat vere an vorse tisas-

Dis fight did last all afternoon—*wohl* to de fesper tide,
Und droo de streeds of Vinchesder, der Breitmann he
    did ride.   [tory !
Vot vears der Breitmann on his hat ? De ploom of fic-
Who's dat a ridin' py his side ? " Dis here's mein son,"
    says he.

How stately rode der Breitmann oop !—how lordly he
    kit down ?   [prown !
How glorious from de great *pokal* he drink de bier so
But der Yunger bick der parrel oop und schwig him
    all at one.   [mein son !"
" Bei Gott ! dat settles all dis dings—I *know* dou art

Der one has got a fader ; de oder found a child.

Bote ride oopon one war-path now in pattle fierce und wild.

It makes so glad our hearts to hear dat dey did so suc-ceed—

Und damit hat sein' Ende DES JUNGEN BREITMANN'S LIED.

Breitmann in Maryland.

DER Breitmann mit his gompany,
  Rode out in Marylandt.
  "Dere's nichts to trink in dis countrie;
Mine troat's as dry as sand.
It's light canteen und haversack,
  It's hoonger mixed mit doorst;
Und if we had some lager-bier
I'd trink oontil I boorst.
  Gling, glang, gloria !
We'd trink oontil we boorst.

" Herr Leut'nant, take a dozen men,
  Und ride dis land around !
Herr Feldwebel, go foragin'
  Dill somedings goot is found.
Gotts-doonder ! men, go ploonder !
  We hafn't trinked a bit
Dis fourdeen hours ! If I had bier
  I'd sauf oontil I shplit !
    Gling, glang, gloria !
    We'd sauf oontil we shplit !"

At mitternacht a horse's hoofs
  Coom rattlin' troo de camp ;
" Rouse dere !—coom rouse der house dere !
  Herr Copitain—we moost tromp !
De scouds have found a repel town,
  Mit repel davern near,
A repel keller in de cround,
  Mit repel lager bier ! !
    Gling, glang, gloria !
    All fool of lager-bier !

Gottsdonnerkreuzschockschwerenoth !
  How Breitmann broked de bush !
" O let me see dat lager bier !
  O let me at him rush !
Und is mein sabre sharp und true,
  Und is mein war-horse goot ?

To get one quart of lager bier
 I'd shpill a sea of ploot.
  Gling, glang, gloria !
 I'd shpill a sea of ploot.

" Fuenf hoonderd repels hold de down,
 One hoonderd strong are we ;
Who gares a tam for all de odds
 Wenn men so dirsty pe."
And in dey smashed and down dey crashed,
 Like donder-polts dey fly,
Rush fort as der wild yæger cooms
 Mit blitzen troo de shky.
  Gling, glang, gloria !
 Like blitzen troo de shky.

How flewed to rite, how flewd to left
 De moundains, drees unt hedge ;
How left und rite de yæger corps
 Went donderin troo de pridge.
Und splash und splosh dey ford de shtream
 Where not some pridges pe :
All dripplin in de moondlight peam
 Stracks went de cavallrie !
  Gling, glang, gloria !
 Der Breitmann's cavallrie.

Und hoory, hoory on dey rote,
　Oonheedin vet or try ;
Und horse und rider shnort und blowed,
　Und shparklin bepples fly.
Ropp ! ropp ! I shmell de barley-prew !
　Dere's somedings goot ish near.
Ropp ! Ropp !—I scent de kneiperei ;
　We've got to lager bier !
　　Gling, glang gloria !
　We've got to lager bier !

Hei ! how de carpine pullets klinged
　Oopon de helmets hart !
Oh, Breitmann—how dy sabre ringed ;
　Du alter Knasterbart !
De contrapands dey sing for choy
　To see de rebs go down,
Und hear der Breitmann grimly gry :
　Hoorah !—we've dook de down.
　　Gling, glang, gloria !
　　Victoria; victoria !
　De Dootch have dook de down.

Mid shout and crash and sabre flash,
　And wild husaren shout
De Dootchmen boorst de keller in,
　Unt rolled de lager out ;

And in the coorlin powder shmoke,
  While shtill de pullets sung.
Dere shtood der Breitmann, axe in hand,
  A knockin out de boong.
    Gling, glang, gloria !
    Victoria ! Encoria !
  De shpicket beats de boong.

Gotts ! vot a shpree der Breitmann had
  While yet his hand was red,
A trinkin lager from his poots
  Among de repel tead.
'Twas dus dey went at mitternight
  Along der moundain side ;
'Twas dus dey help make history !
  Dis was der Breitmann's ride.
    Gling, glang, gloria ;
    Victoria ! Victoria !
    Cer'visia, encoria ?
  De treadful mitnight ride
Of Breitmann's wild Freischarlinger,
  All famous, broad, und wide.

Breitmann as a Bummer.

D ER Sheneral Sherman holts oop on his coorse.
He shtops at de gross-road und reins in his horse.
"Dere's a ford on de rifer dis day we moost dake,
Or elshe de grand army in bieces shall preak!"
Ven shoost ash dis vord from his lips had gone bast,
There coomed a young orterly gallopin fast,
Who gry mit amazement: "Here Shen'ral! Goot Lord!
Dat bummer der Breitmann ish holdin der ford!"

Der Shen'ral he ootered no hymn und no psalm,
But opened his lips und he priefly say " D——n !
Dere moost hafe been viskey on dat side der rifer;
To get it dose shaps would set hell in a shiver,
But now dat dey hold it, ride quick to deir aid :
Ho Sickles ! move promp'ly, send down a prigade
Dat Dootchman moost work mighty hard mit his sword
If againsd a whole army he holds to de ford."

Dey spoored on, dey hoory'd on, gallopin shtraight,
But for Breitmann help coomed shust a liddle too late,
For ash de Lauwiné goes smash mit her pound,
So on to de Bummers de repels coom down :
Heinrich von Schinkenstein's tead in de road,
Dieterich Hinkelbein's flat ash a toad ;
Und Sepperl—Tyroler—shpoke nefer a vord,
But shoost "*Mutter Gottes !*"—und died in de ford.

(17)

Itsch'l of Innspruck ish drilled troo de hair,
  Einer aus Bœblingen—he too vash dere—
Karli of Karlisruh's shot near de fence,
  (His horse vash o'erloadet mit toorkies und hens,)
Und dough he like a ravin mad cannibal fought,
  Yet der Breitmann–der capt'n–der hero vash caught;
Und de last dings ve saw, he was tied mit a cord,
  For de repels had goppled him oop at de ford.

Dey shtripped off his goat und skyugled his poots,
  Dey dressed him mit rags of a repel recruits;
But von grey-haared oldt veller shmiled crimly und bet
  Dat Breitman vouldt pe a pad egg for dem, yet.
" He has more on his pipe as dem vellers allows;
  He has cardts yet in hand und *das Spiel ist nicht aus*,
Dey'll find dat dey took in der teufel to board,
  De day dey pooled Breitmann well ofer de ford."

In de Bowery each bier-haus mit crape vas oop-done,
  Ven dey read in de bapers dat Breitmann vas gone;
Und de Dootch all cot troonk oopon lager und wein,
  At the great Trauer-fest of de Toorner Verein
Dere vas wein-en mit weinen ven beoples did dink
  Dat Sherman's great Sherman cood nefer more trink.
Und in Villiam Shtreet veepin und vailen vas hoor'd,
  Pecause der Hans Breitmann vas lost at de ford.

SECONDT PARDT.

N dulce jubilo now ve all sings,
  A-waivin de panners like avery dings.
De preeze troo de bine-drees ish cooler und salt,
  Und der Shen'ral is merry venefer ve halt;
Loosty und merry he schmells at de preeze,
  Lustig und heiter he looks troo de drees,
Lustig und heiter ash vell he may pe,
  For Sherman, at last, has marched down to the sea!

Dere's a gry from de guart--dere's a clotter und dramp,
  Ven dat fery same orterly rides troo de camp,
Who report on de ford. Dere ish droples and awe
  In de face of de youf' apout somedings he saw;
Und he shpeak me in Fræntsch, like he always do:
  " Look !   [his spook !
Sagre pleu! fentre Tieu!—dere ish Breitmann—
He ish goming dis way! *Nom de garce!* can it pe
  Dat de spooks of te tead men coom down to de sea !"

Und ve looks, und ve sees, und ve tremples mit tread,
  For risin' all swart on de efenin red
Vas Johannes—der Breitmann—der war es, bei Gott!
  Coom ridin to oos-ward, right shtrait to de shpot !
All mouse-still ve shtood, yet mit oop-shoompin hearts,
  For he look shoost so pig ash de shiant of de Hartz;
Und I heard de Sout Deutschers say "Ave Morie !
  Braise Gott all goot shpirids py land und py sea !"
(19)

Boot Itzig of Frankfort he lift oop his nose,
    Und be-mark dat de shpook hat peen changin his
      clothes,
For he seemed like an Generalissimus drest
    In a vlamin new coat and magnificent vest.
Six bistols beschlagen mit silber he wore,
    Und a gold mounted swordt like an Kaisar he bore,
Und ve dinks dat de ghosdt—or votever he pe—
    Moost hafe proken some panks on his vay to de sea.

" Id is he !" "*Und er lebt noch !* he lifes," ve all say :
    Der Breitmann—Oldt Breitmann !—Hans Breit-
      mann ! *Herr Je !*"
Und ve roosh to emprace him, and shtill more ve find
    Dat vherefer he'd peen, he'd left noding pehind.
In bote of his poots dere vas porte-moneys crammed,
    Mit creen-packs stoof full all his haversack jammed,
In his bockets cold dollars were shinglin' deir doons
    Mit two doozen votches und four doozen shpoons,
Und dwo silber tea-pods for makin' his dea,
    Der ghosdt hafe pring mit him, *en route* to de sea.

Mit goot sweed-botatoes, und doorkies, und rice,
    Ve makes him a sooper of avery dings nice.
Und de bummers hoont roundt apout, *alle wie ein*,
    Dill dey findt a plantaschion mit parrels of wein.

Den t'vas " here's to you, Breitmann ! Alt Schwed'—
  bist zuruck ?
  Vot teufels you makes since dis fourteen nights
    week ?"
Und ve holds von shtupendous und derriple shpree
  For choy dat der Breitmann has got to de sea.

But in fain tid ve ashk vhere der Breitmann hat peen,
  Vot he tid ; vot he pass troo—or vot he might seen ?
Vhere he kits his vine horse, or who gafe him dem
    woons,
Und how Brovidence plessed him mit tea-pods und
    shpoons ?
For to all of dem queeries he only reblies
  " If you dells me no quesdions, I ashks you no lies !"
So 'twas glear dat some derriple mysh'dry moost pe
  Vhere he kits all dat ploonder he prings to de sea.

Dere ish bapers in Richmond dells derriple lies
  How Sherman's grand armee hafe raise deir sooplies :
For ve readt *in brindt* dat der Sheneral Grant
  Say de bummers hafe only shoost dake vat dey vant.
But 'tis vhispered dat vhile a refolfer'll go round
  Der BREITMANN vill nefer a peggin' be found ;
Or shtarvin' ash brisner—by doonder !—not he,
  Vhile der teufel could help him to ged to de sea.

Breitmann in Kansas.

V ONCE oopon a dimes, goot vhile afder der war vas ofer, der Herr Breitmann vent oud West, drafellin apout like afery dings—"*circuivit terram et perambulavit eam*," ash der Tyfel said ven dey ask him : "how vash you and how you has peen ?" Von efenings he vas drafel mit some ladies und shendlemans, und he shtaid *incognitus*. Und dey singed songs, dill py und py one of de ladies say : "Ish any podics here ash know de crate pallad of Hans Breitmann's Barty?" Den Hans say : "*Ecce Gallus!* I am dat rooster!" Den der Hans dook a trink und a let-bencil und a biece of baper, and goes indo himself a little dimes und denn coomes out again mit dis boem :

> Hans Breitmann vent to Kansas ;
> He drafel fast und far.
> He rided shoost drei dousand miles
> All in von rail-roat car.
> He knowed foost rate how far he goed—
> He gounted all de vile.
> Dere vash shoost one bottle of champagne,
> Dat bopped at efery mile.

> Hans Breitmann vent to Kansas ;
> I dell you vot my poy.
> You bet dey hat a pully dimes
> In crossin Illinoy.

Dey speaked dere speaks to all de folk
  A shtandin in de car;
Den ask dem in to dake a trink,
  Und corned em *ganz und gar.*

Hans Breitmann vent to Kansas;
  By shings! dey did it prown.
Ven he cot into Leafenvort,
  He found himself in town.
Dey dined him at de Blanter's House,
  More goot as man could dink;
Mit avery dings on eart to eat,
  Und dwice as mooch to trink.

Hans Breitmann vent to Kansas;
  He vent it on de loud.
At Ellsvort, in de prairie land,
  He foundt a pully crowd.
He looked for bleedin' Kansas,
  But dat's "blayed out," dey say;
De whisky keg's de only dings
  Dat's bleedin' der to-day.

Hans Breitmann vent to Kansas,
  To see vot he could hear.
He foundt soom Deutschers dat exisdt
  Py makin' lager bier.

Says he: "*Wie gehts du Alt Gesell?*"
But no dings could be heard;
Dey'd growed so fat in Kansas
Dat dey couldn't speak a vord.

Hans Breitmann vent to Kansas;
Py shings! I dell you vot.
Von day he met a crisly bear
Dat rooshed him down, *bei Gott!*
Boot der Breitmann took und bind der bear,
Und bleased him fery much—
For efery vordt der crisly growled
Vas goot Bavarian Dutch!

Hans Breitmann vent to Kansas!
By donder dat is so!
He ridet out upon de plains
To shase de boofalo.
He fired his rifle at the bools,
Und gallop troo de shmoke,
Und shoomp de canyons shoost as if
Der tyfel vas a choke!

It's hey de trail to Santa Fe;
It's ho! agross de plain.
It's lope along de Denver road,
Until we toorn again.

Und de railroad dravel after us
    Apout as quick as we ;
Dis Kansas ish de fastest land
    Ash efer I did see.

Hans Breitmann vent to Kansas ;
    He have a pully dime ;
Bu 'tvas in oldt Missouri
    Dat dey rooshed him up sublime.
Dey took him to der Bilot Nob,
    Und all der nobs around ;
Dey spreed him und dey tea'd him
    Dill dey roon him to de ground.

Hans Breitmann vent to Kansas ;
    Troo all dis earthly land,
A vorkin out life's mission here
    Soobyectifly und grand.
Some beoblesh runs de beautiful,
    Some works philosophic ;
Der Breitmann solf's de infinide
    Ash von eternal shpree !

Die Schœne Wittwe.

(DE POOTY VIDDER.)

Vot de Yankee Chap sung.

" OAT pooty liddle vidder
    Vot we dosh'nt vish to name,
  Ish still leben on dat liddle shtreet,
A-doin' shuss de same.
De glerks aroundt de gorners
  Somedimes goes round to zee
How die tarlin liddle vitchy ees,
  Und ask 'er how she pe.
Dey lofes her ver' goot liquœr,
  Dey lofes her liddle shtore;
Dey lofes her liddle paby,
  But dey lofes die vidder more.
To dalk mit dat shveet vidder,
  Veu she hands das lager round,
Vill make der shap dat does id
  Pe happy, ve'll be pound.
Dat ish if ve can vell pelieve
  De glerks vat drinks das peer,
Who goes in dere for noding elshe,
  Put simply for to zee her."

(26)

How der Breitmann cut him out.

O ii yes I know die wittwe,
  Mit eyes so prite und proun!
  She's de allerschœnste wittwe
Vot live in dis here town.
In her plack silk gown—mine grashious!—
  All puttoned to de neck—
Und a pooty liddle collar,
  Mitout a shpot or shpeck.
Ho! clear de drack you oder *fraus*—
  You cant pegin to shine
Ven de lofely vidder cooms along—
  Dis vidder ash ish mine!
Ho! clear de drack you Yankee chaps,
  You Englishers und sooch.
You cant pegin to coot me out,
  Mit out you dalks in Dootch.
Ich hab die schœne wittwe
  Schon lange nit geschn,
Ich sah sie gestern Abend
  Wohl bei dem Counter stehn.
Die Wangen rein wie Milch und Blut,
  Die Augen hell und klar.
Ich hab sie sechsmal auch gekusst—
  Potztausend! das ist wahr.

Breitmann and the Turners.

HANS BREITMANN choined de Turners
    Novemper in de fall,
    Und dey gifed a boostin' bender
All in de Toorner Hall.
Dere coomed de whole Gesangverein
    Mit der Liederlich Acpfel Chor,
Und dey blowed on de drooms und stroomed
        on de fifes
    Till dey couldn't refife no more.

Hans Breitmann choined de Toorners,
    Dey all set oop some shouts,
Dey took'd him into deir Toorner Hall,
    Und poots him a course of shprouts,
Dey poots him on de barrell-hell pars
    Und shtands him oop on his head,
Und dey poomps de beer mit an enchine hose
    In his mout' dill he's 'pout half tead !

Hans Breitmann choined de Toorners ;—
    Dey make shimnastig dricks
He stoot on de middle of de floor,
    Und put oop a fifdy-six.
Und den he trows it to de roof,
    Und schwig off a treadful trink :
De veight coom toomple pack on his headt,
    Und py shinks ! he didn't vink !

Hans Breitmann choined de Toorners:—
  Mein Gott! how dey drinked und shwore
Dere vas Schwabians und Tyrolers,
  Und Bavarians by de score.
Some vellers coomed from de Rheinland,
  Und Frankfort-on-de-Main,
Boot dere vas only von Sharman dere,
  Und *he* vas a *Holstein* Dane.

Hans Breitmann choined de Toorners,
  Mit a Limpurg' cheese he coom;
Ven he open de box it schmell so loudt
  It knock de musik doomb.
Ven de Deutschers kit de flavor,
  It coorl de haar on dere head;
Boot dere vas dwo Amerigans dere;
  Und, py tam! it kilt dem dead!

Hans Breitmann choined de Toorners;
  De ladies coomed in to see;
Dey poot dem in de blace for de gals,
  All in der gal-lerie.
Dey ashk: "Vhere ish der Breitmann?"
  And dey dremple mit awe and fear
Ven dey see him schwingen py de toes,
  A trinken lager bier.

Hans Breitmann choined de Toorners:—
    I dells you vot py tam!
Dey sings de great Urbummellied:
    De holy Sharman psalm.
Und ven dey kits to de gorus
    You ought to hear dem dramp!
It scared der Teufel down below
    To hear de Dootchmen stamp.

Hans Breitmann choined de Toorners:—
    By Donner! it vas grand,
Vhen de whole of dem goes a valkin'
    Und dancin' on dere hand,
Mit de veet all wavin' in de air,
    Gottstausend! vot a dricks!
Dill der Breitmann fall und dey all go down
    Shoost like a row of bricks.

Hans Breitmann choined de Toorners,
    Dey lay dere in a heap,
And slept dill de early sonnen shine
    Come in at de window creep;
And de preeze it vake dem from deir dream,
    And dey go to kit deir feed:
Here hat' dis song an Ende—
    Das ist DES BREITMANNSLIED.

Ballad.

DER noble Ritter Hugo
　　Von Schwillensaufenstein,
　　Rode out mit shpeer and helmet,
　　Und he coom to de panks of de Rhine.

Und oop dere rose a meer maid,
　　Vot hadn't got nodings on,
Und she say, "Oh, Ritter Hugo,
　　Vhere you goes mit yourself alone?"

And he says, "I rides in de creenwood
　　Mit helmet und mit shpeer,
Till I cooms into em Gasthaus,
　　Und dere I trinks some beer."

Und den outshpoke de maiden
　　Vot hadn't got nodings on:
"I tont dink mooch ol beoplesh
　　Dat goes mit demselfs alone.

"You'd petter coom down in de wasser,
　　Vere deres heaps of dings to see,
Und hafe a shplendid tinner
　　Und drafel along mit me.
　　　　31)

" Dere you sees de fisch a schwimmin,
    Und you catches dem efery one :"—
So sang dis wasser maiden
    Vot hadn't got nodings on.

" Dere ish drunks all full mit money
    In ships dat vent down of old;
Und you helpsh yourself, by dunder!
    To shimmerin crowns of gold.

" Shoost look at dese shpoons und vatches!
    Shoost see dese diamant rings!
Coom down und full your bockets,
    Und I'll giss you like avery dings.

" Vot you vantsh mit your schnapps und lager?
    Coom down into der Rhine!
Der ish pottles der Kaiser Charlemagne
    Vonce filled mit gold-red wine!"

Dat fetched him—he shtood all shpell pound;
    She pooled his coat-tails down,
She drawed him oonder der wasser,
    De maidens mit nodings on.

Hans Breitmann's Christmas.

"Hæc est illa bona dies   "Nullus metus, nec labores,
Et vocata læta quies   Nulla cura, nec dolores,
Vina sitientibus.   Sint in hoc symposio."

[De Generibus Ebriosorum, Francoforti ad Mœnum, A. D. 1565.]

ID vas on Weihnachtsabend—vot Ghristmas Efe dey
 call—
Der Breitmann mit his Breitmen tid rent de Musik
 Hall ;
Ash de Breitmen und die romen who were in de Lie-
 derkranz
Vouldt plend deir souls in harmonie to have a bleasin
 tantz.

Dey reefed de Hall 'mid pushes so nople to be seen,
Aroundt Beethoven's buster dey on-did a garlandt creen ;
De laties vork like tyfels two days to scroob de vloor,
Und hanged a crate serenity mit Willkomm ! oop de toor !

Und vhile dere vas a Schwein-blatt whose redakteur tid
 say :
Dat Breitmann he vas liederlich vet antworded dis away,
Ve maked anoder serenity mid ledders plue und red :
" Our Leader lick de repels ! N. G." (enof gesaid.)

Und anoder serene dransparency ve make de veller
 baint,
Boot de vay he potch und vertyfeled it vas enof to
 shvear a saint,

(33)

For ve vantcd La Germania—boot der ardist mit a
    bloonder
Vent und vlorished Lager agross id—und denn poot
    Mania oonder !

Und as Ghristmas Efe was gekommen de beoples weren
    im Hall,
I shvears you id vas Gott-full—dat shplendit, pe-glo-
    ried ball?
Ve hat foon wie der Teufel in Frankreich—we coot oop
    like ter tyfel in France,
Und valk pair-wise in, while de musik blayed loudt de
    Fackel-Tanz.

But ven de valtz shtrike oopwart we most went out of fits,
Ash der Breitmann led off on a dwister mid de lofely
    Helmina Schmitz.
He valtz shoost like he vas shtandin shtill, mit a peau-
    diful solemn shmile,
Und 'Mina say he nafer shtop poussiren allaweil.

"Es tœnt, es rauschet Saitenklang—I hear de musik
    call
Den kerzenhellen Saal entlang—all troo de gleamin
    Hall,
O mœcht ich schweben stolz und froh—O mighdt I
    efer pe
Mit dir durchs ganze Leben so !—my Lebenlang by dee."

Und faster play de musik de Wellen und Wogen von
    Strauss ;

Und some drop into de tantzen und some of dem drop
    aus ;

Und soon like a shtorm in de Meere I feel de reelin vloor,

So de shpinners shtop mit de shpinsters, for dey couldn't
    shpin no more.

Now weren ve all frolic, und lauter guter ding,

Und dirsty ash a broosh-pinder—ven ve hear some
      glœsses ring ;

Foorst mild und sonft in de distants—like de song of a
    nightingoll,

Den a ringin und rottlin und clotterin—ash de Gluck
    of Edenhall ?

Hei ! how we roosh on de liquor !—hei ! how de kell-
    ners coom !

Hei ! how we busted de bier kegs und poonished de
    Punsch a la Rhum,

Like lonely wafes at mitternight oopon some shiant
    shore ;

Like an awful shtorm in de Wælder—was de dirsty
    Deutschers' roar !

I pyed some carts for a dime abiece—I pyed shoost
    fifdy-dwo.

Dey were goot for bier, or schnapps, or wein—py don-
    der how dey flew!

I ring de deck on de vaiters for liquor hot und cool,
Und avery dime I blays a cart, py shings, I rake de
pool !

Und ash ve trinked so comforble, like boogs in any roog,
De trompets blowed *tan da ra dei*, und dere coom in a
Maskenzug,
A peaudiful brocession, soul-raisin und sooplime,
De marmorbilds of de heroes of de early Sherman dime.

Dere vent der gross Arminius, mit his frau Thusnelda,
too,
De vellers ash lam de Romans dill dey roon mit noses
pluc,
Den vollowed Quinctilius Varus, who carry a Roman
yoke,
Und arm-in-arm mit Gambrinus come der Allemane
Chroe.

Der alte Friedrich Rothbart, und Kaiser Karl der crate,
Mit Roland und Uliverus ven shveepin on in shtate ;
Und Conradin whose sad-full deat' shtill makes our
heartsen pleed,
Und all of dem oldt vellers aus dem Niblungen Lied.

Und as dey mofed on, der Breitmann maked a tyfeled
shplendid witz
In anti-word to dis quesdion from de lofely 'Mina
Schmitz :

" Vy ish id dey always makes in shtone dem rollers so
andiquatet ?"

" Vy—dey set in de laps of Ages dill dey got lapi-
dated !"

Und shoost ash de last of dis hisdory hat fonished troo
de toor,
Ve heardt a ge-screech, und Pelz Nickel coom howlin
on de vloor ;
Den de laties yell like der tyfel, und vly like gulls mit
vings,
Und der Peltz Nickel lick em mit svitches und ve
laughed like averydings.

I nefer hafe sooch laughen before dat I was geborn,
Und Pelz Nickel ven 'twas ober he blow ou a yæger horn
Und denounce do all de beople gesembled in de hall :
Dat a Ghristmas dree vas vaiten mit bresents for oos all !

So ve vollowed him into de zimmer so quick ash dese
vords he said,
To kit dem peaudiful bresents, all gratis und on de dead,
Und in faedt a shplendid Weihnachtsbaum mid lighds
ve druly found,
Und liddel kifts da' ge-kostet a benny abicce all round!

Dere vas Rika Stange die Dessauerinn—a maedchen
shtraigdt und tall,
She got a bicture of Cupid—boot she didn't see it at all

Dill der Breitmann say mit his shplendid shtyle dat all
    de laties dake :
"Dat pend of de bow is de Crecian pend dat you so
    ofden make !"

Anoder scharmante laty, Maria Top, did got
A schwingin mid a ribbon, a liddle benny pot;
Boot Breitmann hafe id de roughest of any oder mans,
For he kit a yellow gratle mit a liddle wooden Hans.

Den next Beethoven's Sinfonie, die orkester did blay ;
Adagio—allegro—andante cantabile.
We sat in shtill commotion so dat a bin mighdt drops,
Und de deers roon town der Breitmann's sheeks mit-
    whiles he was trinkin schnapps.

Next dings ve had de Weinnachtstraum gesung by de
    Liederkranz.
Denn I trinked dwelf schoppens of glee wine to sed me
    oop for a tanz ;
Dis dimes I tanz wie der Tyfel—we shriek de volk on
    de vloor ;
Und boost right indo de sooper room—for ve tanzt a
    hole troo de door !

Denn 'twas rowdy tow und hop-sossa, ve hollered, Mann
    und Weib ;
"Rip Sam und sed her oop acain !—ve're all of de
    Shackdaw tribe !"

Venn Pelz Nickel blow his trump once more, und peg
    peg oos to shtop our din,
Und troo de open toor dere comed nine denpins
    marchin in.

Nine vellers tressed like denpins—dey goed to der end'
    der hall,
Und dwo Hans Wurst, shack-puddin glowns—dey rolled
    at em mit a pall.
De palls vas painted peaudiful; dey vas vifdeen feet
    aroundt;
Und de rule of de came : whoefer cot hidt moost doom-
    ple on de croundt.

Somedimes dey hit de denpins—somedimes de oder
    volk—
Und pooty soon de gompany was all laid out in shoke ;
Boot I tells you vot it makes oos laugh dill ve py nearly
    shplits,
Ven der Breitmann he roll ofer and drip up de Mina
    Schmitz.

Dis lets itself in Sherman pe foost-rade word-blayed on,
Und mongst oos be giftet vellers you pet dat it vas tone!
How der Breitmann mighdt drafel as brideman on de
    roadt dat ish *breit* and *krumm ;*
Here de drumpets soundt, and pair-wise ve goed for de
    sooper room.

Ve goed for ge-roasted Welsh-hens, ve goed for ge-
spickter hare,
Ve goed for kartoffel salade mit butter brod—Kaviar;
Ve roosh at de lordtly sauer-kraut und de wurst vich
lofely shine,
Und oh mein Gott in Kimmel! how we goed for de
Mosel-wein!

Und troonker more, und troonker yet, und troonker shtill
got ve,
In rosy lighdt shtill drivin on agross a fairy see;
Den madder, wilder, frantic-er I proked a salat dish!
Und shoost like roarin elefants ve tanzt aroundt de tish.

I'fe shvimmed in heafenly troonks pefore—boot nefer
von like dis,
De morgen-het-ache only seemt a bortion of de bliss.
De while in trilling peauty roundt like heafenly vind-
harps rang
A goosh of golden melodie — de Rhineweinbechers
Klang.

De meltin minnesingers song—a droonk of honeyd
rhyme—
De b'wildrin-dipsy Bardic shants of Teutoburgic dime,
Back to de runic dim Valhall und Balder's foamin
mead;
——Here ents in heller glorie schein des Breitmann's
Weihnachtslied!

Schnitzerl's Philosopede.

HERR SCHNITZERL make a philosopede,
  Von of de pullyest kind;
It vent mitout a vheel in front,
And hadn't none pehind.
Von vheel vas in de mittel, dough,
  And it vent as sure as ecks,
For he shtraddled on de axle dree
  Mit de vheel petween his lecks.

Und ven he vant to shtart id off
  He paddlet mit his veet,
Und soon he cot to go so vast
  Dat avery dings he peat.
He run her out on Broader shtreed,
  He shkeeted like der vind,
Hei! how he bassed de vancy crabs,
  And lef dem all pehind!

De vellers mit de trottin nags
  Pooled oop to see him bass;
De Deutschers all erstaunished saidt:
  "*Potztausend! Was ist das?*"
Boot vaster shtill der Schnitzerl flewed
  On—mit a gashtly smile;
He tidn't tooch de dirt, py shings!
  Not vonce in half a mile.

(41)

Oh, vot ish all dis eartly pliss?
Oh, vot ish man's soocksess?
Oh, vot ish various kinds of dings?
Und vot ish hobbiness?
Ve find a pank-node in de shtreedt,
Next dings der pank is preak;
Ve folls, und knocks our outsides in,
Ven ve a ten shtrike make.

So vas it mit der Schnitzerlein
On his philosopede.
His feet both shlipped outsideward shoost
Vhen at his extra shpeed.
He felled oopon der vheel of course;
De vheel like blitzen flew:
Und Schnitzerl he vas schnitz in vact
For id shlished him grod in two.

Und as for his philosopede,
Id cot so shkared, men say,
It pounded onward till it vent
Ganz teufelwards afay.
Boot vhere ish now de Schnitzerl's soul?
Vhere dos his shbirit pide?
In Himmel troo de entless plue,
It takes a medeor ride.

Der Freischuetz.

WIE geht's my frients—if you'll allow,
　　I sings you rite avay shoost now
　　Some dretful shdories vitch dey calls
DER FREYSCHUETZ; or, de Magic Balls.

Wohl in Bohemian land it cooms,
Where folks trinks prandy mate of plums;
Dere lifed ein Yager—Maxerl Schmit,
Who shot mit goons and nefer hit.

Und dere vas one old Yager, who
Says, " Maxerl, dis vill nefer do;
If you should miss on trial day,
Dere'l pe de tyfel den to pay.

" If you do miss, you shtupid goose,
Dere'l pe de donnerwetter loose;
For you shant have mine taughter's hand,
Nor pe de Hertshog's yagersmann."

It coomed pefore de day was set,
Dat all de chaps togeder met,
Und Maxerl fired his bix and missed,
Und all de gals cot round and hissed.

Dey laughed pefore, and hissed pehind;
Put one chap, Kaspar, set : "tont mind!
I dells you what, you stuns 'em alls,
If yoost you shoot mit magic palls."

"De magic palls—oh vot is dat !"
"I got dem in mine hoontin hat ;
De're plack as kohl und shoot so true,
Oh dems de sort of palls for you.

"You see dat eagle flyin high,
Ein hoondred miles up in de sky?
Shoot at dat eagle mit your bix,
You kills him dead as doonderblix."

"I tont pelieve de dings you say."
"You fool," says Kass, "den plaze avay !"
He plazed avay, ven sure as blood,
Down coomed de eagle in de mud.

"*O was ist das?*" said Maxerl Schmit,
"Vy—dat's de eagle vat you hit.
You kills um vhen you plaze avay ;
But dat's a ting you nix ferstay.

"Und you moost go to make dem balls
To de Wolf's Glen ven mitnight falls ;
Dow knowst de shpot?—alone and late"—
"O ja—I knows him *ganz* foost-rate."

" But denn I does not likes to go
Among dem dings." Says Kass, "Ach sho!
I'll help you fix dem tyfel chaps;
Like a goot fellow—take some schnapps!

"(*Hilf Zamiel! hilf!*)—Here, trink some more!"
Den Kass vent shtomping roundt de floor,
Und coomed his hoomboogs ofer Schmit,
Till Max said "*Nun—ich gehe mit!*"

All in de finster mitternockt,
When oder folks in shleep vas locked,
Down in de *Wolfsschlucht* Kass did try
His tyfel-strikes und *hexerei*.

Mit skools and pones he made a ring,
De howls and spooks pegin to sing;
Und all de tyfels oonter ground
Coome breaking loose and rushin round.

Den Maxerl cooms along; says he,
" Mein Gott! what dings is dis I see!
I dinks de fery tyfel und all
Moost help to make dem magic pall.

" I vish dat I had nix cum rous,
Und shtaid mineself in bett to house."
"*Hilf Zamiel!*" cried Kass, " you whelp!
You red Dootch tyfel—coom und help!"

Den up dere coomed a tredful shtorm,
De todtengrips aroundt did schwarm;
De howl joomped oop und flapt his vings,
Und turned his het like averydings.

Up troo de groundt here coomed a pot,
Mit leadt und dings to make de shot;
Und hœllisch fire in crimson plaze,
Und awful schmells like Schweitzer kæs'.

Across de scene a pine shtick flew,
Mit seferal jail-pirds fastent to,
Six treadful jail-birds, mit deir vings
Tied to de shticks mit magic shtrings.

All troo de air, all in a row,
Die wilde Jagd was seen to go;
De hounts und deer all made of pone,
Und hoonted by a skilleton.

Dere coomed de dretful shpectre pig
Who shpitten fire, away did dig;
Und fiery drocks und tyfel-snake
A scootin troo de air tid preak.

But Kass he tidn't mind dem alls,
But casted out de pullet palls;
Six was to go as dey wouldt like,
De sevent moost for de tyfel strike.

At last oopon de trial day
De gals coomed round so nice and gay ;
Und denn dey goes and makes a tanz
Und stinged apout de *Jungfernkranz.*

Und denn der Hertshog—dat's de Duke—
Cooms down und dinks he'll take a look ;
"Young mans," to Maxerl denn says he,
"Shoost shoot dem dove upon dat dree !"

Denn Maxerl pointed mit de bix—
"Potzblitz !" says he, " dat dove I'll fix !"
He fired his rifle at de *Taub,*
When Kass rolled over in de *Staub.*

De pride she falled too in de dust,
De gals dey cried—de men dey cussed :
De Hertshog says, "It's fery clear
Dat dere has peen some tyfels here ;

"Und Max has shot mit tyfels-*blei.*
Pfui!—die verfluchte Hexerei !
O Maximilian !   O du
Gehst nit mit rechten Dingen zu !"

But den a hermits coomed in late,
Says he, "I'll fix dese dings foost-rate."
Und telld de Hertshog dat young men
Will raise der tyfel now and denn.

De Duke forgifed de Kaspar dann
Und made of him ein Yagersmann,
What shoots mit bixen gun and pfeil,
Und talks apout de *Waidmannsheil.*

Und denn de pride she coomed to life,
Und cot to pe de Maxerl's wife ;
Den all de beoples cried Hoorah !
Das ist recht brav ! und hopsasa !

THE END.